This We Believe: Successful Schools for Young Adolescents

This We Believe:
Successful Schools for Young Adolescents

A Position Paper of
National Middle School Association

National Middle School Association
Westerville, Ohio

National Middle School Association
4151 Executive Parkway, Suite 300
Westerville, Ohio 43081
Telephone: (800) 528-NMSA
www.nmsa.org

NMSA

Printed in the United States of America.

Sue Swaim, Executive Director
Jeff Ward, Associate Executive Director
Edward Brazee, Editor, Professional Publications
John Lounsbury, Consulting Editor, Professional Publications
April Tibbles, Director of Publications
Dawn Williams, Production Specialist
Mark Shumaker, Graphic Designer
Mary Mitchell, Designer, Editorial Assistant
Marcia Meade-Hurst, Senior Publications Representative

The sub-title of this paper, *Successful Schools for Young Adolescents,* was the title of a book published by Transaction Publishers in 1983. Permission to use it in this work was graciously granted by the author, Joan Lipsitz, and the publisher.

Library of Congress Cataloging-in-Publication Data
This we believe: successful schools for young adolescents: a position paper of
    National Middle School Association.
        p. cm
    ISBN 1-56090-142-X (pbk.)
    1. Middle schools--United States. I. National Middle School Association
LB1623.5.T55 2003
373.2'36--dc22

                                                2003044251

National Middle School Association's position paper should be a living document, fully able to reflect our philosophy and understanding of young adolescents and the conditions that make effective middle level schools. Therefore, the association's board of trustees authorized an extensive review process that resulted in this third edition, now entitled *This We Believe: Successful Schools for Young Adolescents.*

Over 250 middle level educators and researchers were invited to review the 1995 position paper and, based upon their experience and knowledge, offer recommendations for changes, additions, or continuation of various aspects of the paper. Additionally, through NMSA's Web site, an invitation went to the more than 30,000 members asking for similar input, thus giving them the unprecedented opportunity to directly participate in revising this important document.

All suggestions received were reviewed by all members of the revision committee. These individuals, Edward Brazee, Deborah Kasak, John Lounsbury, Gert Nesin, Charles Palmer, Linda Robinson, Sue Swaim, and Phyllis Toy Wong are to be commended for their work on this important professional task. The contribution of Peter Scales who provided the research-based listing of characteristics is gratefully acknowledged, and a special word of thanks goes to Chris Stevenson for his insightful review and encouragement to make the document "sing." Long-time editor, John Lounsbury, is owed enduring gratitude for his continuing commitment to the implementation of successful middle level schools. He, along with Ed Brazee, spent many hours of thoughtful and visionary reflection and refinement that has helped to bring this well-crafted document to life.

Sue Swaim, Executive Director
National Middle School Association

Contents

Preface

The history of middle level or intermediate education spans a century. In the early days of the junior high school movement, 1910-1925, several widely recognized position statements set forth the goals and responsibilities of this fledgling American institution. Then in 1947 the six functions of the junior high school proposed by Gruhn and Douglass became the standard as efforts were made to revitalize the junior high school. However, following the introduction of the middle school in the 1960s, no single comprehensive statement appeared to crystallize the educational beliefs inherent in this emerging educational reform effort.

Recognizing the need for clarification and direction, John Swaim, the 1980 president of National Middle School Association, appointed a committee to prepare a position paper. That committee, chaired by Alfred A. Arth, included William Alexander, Charles Cherry, Donald Eichhorn, Conrad Toepfer, and Gordon Vars. After a period of many months and numerous drafts, preliminary papers were submitted to John Lounsbury for refinement, editing, and publication. The final board-approved document, *This We Believe,* was published in 1982.

Following its release, this paper had a far-reaching impact on middle level education. It quickly became the most frequently cited statement about the education of young adolescents and was reprinted seven times to meet the demand for its content. In 1992, the paper was reissued in a fresh format and subsequently reprinted five more times.

The first edition of *This We Believe* more than fulfilled the need for professional guidelines, and it holds a place of importance in the literature of middle level education. However, developments in education and in the practice of middle level education in particular were so extensive that in 1994 the association recognized the need to revisit its position paper. Committee members charged with this responsibility were: John Arnold, Sherrel Bergmann, Barbara Brodhagen, Ross Burkhardt, Maria Garza-Lubeck, John Lounsbury, Marion Payne, Chris Stevenson, Sue Swaim, and Gordon Vars. The second edition was not just a revision, but a re-vision of middle level education, one that more fully expressed the association's beliefs as the 21st century approached. Intensive committee discussions, and numerous drafts incorporating suggestions received from board members and other active middle level educators led to the final document that was unanimously approved by NMSA's Board of Trustees in September 1995.

The more than 350,000 copies distributed have been used by entire middle school faculties, parent groups, boards of education, and school districts, making *This We Believe* the most widely used document on middle level education ever published. Schools have employed it as criteria for school evaluations, self-studies, parent and public education initiatives, and future planning. A series of position papers, research and curriculum summaries, and many research studies have been based on or derived from it.

Although only seven years passed since the second edition of *This We Believe* was revised, significant events made another rewrite imperative. In 2002 the following committee members were charged with the task of reviewing, revising, and rewriting as necessary the association's position paper: Edward Brazee, Deborah Kasak, John Lounsbury, Gert Nesin, Charles Palmer, Linda Robinson, Sue Swaim, and Phyllis Toy Wong.

As before, this edition is the result of intensive discussions, the suggestions of board members and others on an early draft, the addition of new sections, many subsequent drafts, and word by word refinements by a subcommittee of Sue Swaim, John Lounsbury, and Edward Brazee.

The positions stated or inferred in *This We Believe: Successful Schools for Young Adolescents* are supported by a burgeoning research base about young adolescent growth and development and successful practices in curriculum, organization, and indeed every aspect of middle level schools. *Research and Resources in Support of This We Believe,* a companion document released concurrently, details this research base.

This We Believe: Successful Schools for Young Adolescents was unanimously approved by the NMSA Board of Trustees in July 2003; it is offered to the profession and the public as a guide to assist in creating successful schools for young adolescents. More than ever before, it is critical that this document be read, understood, and used by students, teachers, parents, policymakers, and other citizens concerned about the education of young adolescents.

"To change the world, teach a young adolescent."

The Importance of
Middle Level Education

Every day, twenty million diverse, rapidly changing 10- to 15-year-olds enrolled in our nation's middle level schools are making critical and complex life choices. They are forming the attitudes, values, and habits of mind that will largely direct their behavior as adults. They deserve schools that support them fully during this key phase of life. Therefore, National Middle School Association seeks to conceptualize and promote successful middle level schools that enhance the healthy growth of young adolescents as lifelong learners, ethical and democratic citizens, and increasingly competent, self-sufficient young people who are optimistic about the future.

For middle schools to be successful, their students must be successful; for students to be successful, the school's organization, curriculum, pedagogy, and programs must be based upon the developmental readiness, needs, and interests of young adolescents. This concept is at the heart of middle level education. In this document, National Middle School Association sets forth a vision to guide the decisions of those responsible for shaping educational programs that are committed to improving both learning and learners.

Contemporary society presents remarkably different challenges from those educators faced just a few decades ago. While the traditional school functions – sharing our national heritage, acquiring fundamental knowledge, teaching the tools of scholarship and the workplace, and promoting democratic citizenship – remain valid, achieving these functions today and meeting the academic imperative and other new responsibilities require relevant curriculum and varied, engaging teaching strategies that complement contemporary students. Middle level educators, therefore, promote schools that build on effective traditional practices as they create schools where learning is both expedient and joyful and where learners are celebrated for their initiative and accomplishments.

When developing successful middle level schools, educators and others must consider the intent of the various concepts, specific programs, or operational features recommended. They should weigh the "spirit" behind any proposal by asking "What is the ultimate purpose of this program?" "What are we trying to accomplish?" or "How will this program affect student growth, development, and achievement?"

Perhaps the most profound and enduring lesson learned in 30 years of active middle school advocacy is that the several distinct elements of successful middle level schools work best as parts of the larger whole. In the early years of the middle school movement, educators implemented what were then seen as middle school characteristics such as advisory programs, teams, and exploratory offerings. While research and cumulative, empirical evidence have confirmed that these characteristics when present over time lead to higher levels of student achievement and are supportive of the middle school concept, they have limited value when implemented singly. Schools should not choose among characteristics, implementing only those that appear to be more achievable or seem more appropriate for a school or a particular situation. Rather, successful middle level schools recognize that the 14 characteristics described in *This We Believe: Successful Schools for Young Adolescents* are interdependent and must be implemented in concert.

> Schools should not choose among characteristics, implementing only those that appear to be more achievable or seem more appropriate for a particular situation.

Young Adolescents

Young people undergo more rapid and profound personal changes between the ages 10 and 15 than at any other time in their lives. Although growth in infancy is also very extensive, infants are not the conscious witnesses of their development. Early adolescence is a period of tremendous variability among youngsters of the same gender and chronological age. Dissimilar rates of growth are common in all areas of their development. Changes occur irregularly, and no two young adolescents enter puberty at the same time or progress at the same rate. Individual differences proliferate, making dubious such assumptions as, "All seventh graders are…." Race, poverty, or ethnicity may play an important role, as these conditions add to the tremendous variability of students. It is vitally important to recognize that the areas of development – intellectual, physical, social, emotional, and moral – are inexorably intertwined. With young adolescents, achieving academic success is highly dependent upon their other developmental needs also being met.

> **With young adolescents, achieving academic success is highly dependent upon their other developmental needs also being met.**

Changes in middle level students' patterns of thinking become evident in the ideas they have about the world and how it functions. These shifts may be apparent through the questions they pose to each other and to trusted adults, in their reflections about personal experiences, in their views on moral issues, and through their perceptions of stories, images, and humor. Young adolescents reveal growing capacity for thinking about how they learn, for considering multiple ideas, and for planning steps to carry out their own learning activities. Such evidence heralds growth toward more mature and abstract ways of thinking. However, because cognitive growth occurs gradually and irregularly, most middle level students require ongoing, concrete, experiential learning in order to develop intellectually.

Early adolescence is characterized by accelerated movement toward reproductive maturity. Hormonal shifts trigger physical transformations such as redistribution of body fat, increases in weight and height, abrupt bone and muscle growth, and changes in voice, hair, and complexion. In general, physical maturation begins much earlier for girls than boys. Sexual development prompts new physical, emotional, and social concerns for both sexes. Early or late physical maturation affects self-perception as well as status with peers and adults.

Concerns about appearance and body image usually generate heightened interest in personal grooming among young adolescents. Yet, their health choices are often inappropriate, for example, eating foods inadequate for meeting the nutritional needs of their changing bodies. In addition, many youngsters begin experimenting with tobacco, alcohol, other harmful drugs, and sex, all of which pose serious, potential threats to personal health. Rapid physical changes combined with the multiple hazards of contemporary life make early adolescence a crucial period for developing healthy personal habits.

Parents or guardians almost always retain primary authority and continue as the source of basic values for children. However, young people's desire for peer acceptance and the need to belong to particular social groups are often intense and sometimes lead to shifting allegiance from adults to peers. Issues of right and wrong, good and bad, appropriate and inappropriate are increasingly influenced by other young adolescents and by the media. Parents should recognize the reticence of young adolescents to communicate with family members as part of their striving for independence. Families, however, should take care to keep their end of the communication line open. At the same time, remember that young adolescents hunger for positive relationships with caring adults and opportunities for informal interactions and conversations with them.

Another concern is the effect of social forces on the moral development of young adolescents. For the most part, young people make good choices, but those decisions become more difficult in a world where violence and the exploitation of vulnerable youth are all too prevalent. Young people receive conflicting messages about sexuality and appropriate behavior, and often their schools and even parents may shy away from discussing such issues with them. Developmentally responsive middle level schools construct curricula that actively assist young people as they formulate positive moral principles. This crucial guidance, of course, must reflect sensitivity and consider family and community expectations.

All in all, the several developmental processes associated with adolescence, while natural and necessary, present challenges to those entrusted with the responsibility for the healthy development and education of young adolescents, and it is very clear that the schools of yesterday are ill-suited for meeting the challenges of today.

The Changing Society

The many transitions individuals undergo during early adolescence would make growing up difficult enough in an unchanging world. Societies today, however, are evolving rapidly, and virtually every aspect of life has been altered. The second half of the 20th century brought about unprecedented changes, especially in gender roles, family structures and traditions, influences of electronic and print media, the increasingly diverse and multicultural nature of communities, and a growing international influence on life. Although modern life is richer in many ways, the roles and markers for youth have become ambiguous, offering fewer opportunities for making meaningful contributions to family or society.

Family structure is also undergoing redefinition. Nuclear and extended families once provided clearer roles and responsibilities, and many still do. However, with diverse family configurations, some young adolescents are growing up in situations that vary in the number, gender, race, or ethnicity of parents or guardians. In addition, far too many children grow up lacking adequate supervision. Without responsible adult role models present, unhealthy situations exist when young adolescents live in an environment rife with temptations.

Although physical maturity occurs earlier than in previous generations, children still confront the same developmental hurdles. During early adolescence they need supportive adult guidance and advocacy as much or more than ever as they struggle to maintain the hope and optimism that have typically characterized youth.

The economy also directly affects young adolescents. A substantial number have considerable disposable income and are a major target of marketing campaigns, most of which are clearly manipulative. Others have little or no disposable money, yet live exposed to the same marketing pressures. Many of the entertainment options available to young adolescents foster superficial and selfish values, depict gender roles inappropriately, and promote a passive, consumer-oriented, and at times, a self-destructive lifestyle. Young adolescents also witness the negative results of poverty, racism, drug and alcohol abuse, crime, and child abuse, often without opportunities to understand why these conditions occur and what they might do about them. Schools and community programs must do more to cultivate responsible, moral decision makers and discriminating, enlightened consumers.

The guidelines for selecting educational goals, curriculum content, and instructional processes grow out of an awareness of and respect for the nature of these distinctive young adolescents. Educators who understand them and the cultural context in which they grow to maturity will make wise decisions about the kinds of schools needed.

The Vision Framed

National Middle School Association's vision for a successful middle school is delineated in the following 14 characteristics. Eight are facets of the culture of such schools. The remaining six are programmatic characteristics that can evolve in such a culture. As previously noted, all of these features or attributes of a successful middle school, while nesessarily presented as individual items, must work in harmony.

National Middle School Association believes...

Successful schools for young adolescents are characterized by a culture that includes

- Educators who value working with this age group and are prepared to do so
- Courageous, collaborative leadership
- A shared vision that guides decisions
- An inviting, supportive, and safe environment
- High expectations for every member of the learning community
- Students and teachers engaged in active learning
- An adult advocate for every student
- School-initiated family and community partnerships.

positive school climate

Therefore, successful schools for young adolescents provide

- Curriculum that is relevant, challenging, integrative, and exploratory
- Multiple learning and teaching approaches that respond to their diversity
- Assessment and evaluation programs that promote quality learning
- Organizational structures that support meaningful relationships and learning
- School-wide efforts and policies that foster health, wellness, and safety
- Multifaceted guidance and support services.

flexible organizational structures

Successful schools for young adolescents are characterized by a culture that includes

Educators who value working with this age group and are prepared to do so.

Effective middle level educators make a conscious choice to work with young adolescents and advocate for them. They understand the developmental uniqueness of this age group, the curriculum they teach, and effective learning and assessment strategies. Such educators are collaborators who know how to form learning partnerships with their students, demonstrating empathy while engaging them in significant academic learning experiences.

Middle level educators have a zest for living; they enjoy being with young adolescents and understand the dynamics of the ever-changing youth culture. They recognize the value of interdisciplinary studies and integrative learning and make sound pedagogical decisions based on the needs, interests, and special abilities of their students. They are sensitive to individual differences, respond positively to the diversity present, and know how to involve families.

Middle level educators serve as role models for students. They realize their own behavior sends influential messages to young adolescents and so practice those qualities of heart and mind they want young adolescents to develop. Educators serve their students well when they model inclusive, collaborative, democratic, and team-oriented approaches to teaching and learning. When such dedicated and knowledgeable middle level educators work together, they create exciting possibilities for all students; their professional commitment and passion make a positive difference in the lives of the young adolescents they teach.

Educators need specific teacher preparation before they enter middle level classrooms and continuous professional development as they pursue their careers. Guidelines and exemplary programs for preparing middle level educators have been published by National Middle School Association and others. Such programs require depth of knowledge in at least two content areas, understanding of the learning process, and extensive field-based experiences at the middle level. State departments of education and institutions of higher learning share responsibility for developing appropriate programs to provide both initial preparation and graduate programs leading to middle level licensure. Schools and school districts have the prime responsibility for providing ongoing professional development but should use the resources provided by state departments, colleges, universities, and professional associations.

Courageous, collaborative leadership

Courageous, collaborative middle level leaders understand young adolescents and the society in which they live. They also understand the theory and best practice of middle level education. As architects for change, such leaders know that yesterday does not have to determine tomorrow. They strive to educate colleagues, parents, policymakers, and community members about middle school philosophy and proven practices in order to build support for long-term, continuous school improvement. Their understanding and commitment help them challenge and change practices that do not serve students' best interests. Such leaders understand the nuances of teaming, student advocacy, and exploration as components of a larger middle level program. Ultimately, such leadership empowers others to make the often needed hard decisions as they address the education and well-being of each and every student.

Central office staff, boards of education, and other stakeholders play important roles in developing successful schools for young adolescents; but clearly, the principal has the central role. As the prime determiner of the school culture, the principal influences student achievement and teacher effectiveness by advocating, nurturing, and sustaining an effective instructional program. The principal, working collaboratively with a leadership team, focuses on building a learning community that involves all teachers and places top priority on the education and healthy development of every student, teacher, and staff member.

Courageous middle level leaders know that professional development should be integrated into the daily life of the school and directly linked to the school's goals for student and teacher success and growth. To meet these goals, people work together in study groups, focus on learning results, analyze student work, and carry out action research. The principal promotes instructional improvement through ongoing informal conversations with teachers about classroom practices as well as by more formal conferences.

Principals understand that successful schools committed to the long-term implementation of the middle school concept must be collaborative enterprises in which improvement does not depend on any single person. Such principals recognize teachers as leaders and use the expertise of a variety of people to ensure the academic growth and well-being of every student. They understand that school reform is a long-term proposition; to be successful, new programs must become integral to the school culture. They also know that the school itself is a teacher and that pupils learn not only from the instruction offered but from the implicit lessons as well – the ways adults treat each other, set priorities, and make decisions.

> **The school itself is a teacher. Pupils learn not only from the instruction offered but from the implicit lessons as well.**

A shared vision that guides decisions

Vision, as someone has said, is an acute sense of the possible. Research and exemplary practice over the past four decades have provided middle level educators with a strong sense of the possible. Idealistic and uplifting, the resulting vision reflects the very best we know and lights the way toward achieving a truly successful middle level school. It reveals how research and practice can work in harmony to provide the foundation for building a school in which every student can succeed. The vision becomes the basis for a concise, written mission statement that is known and supported by all stakeholders – students, teachers, administrators, families, board of education members, and others in the community.

The collaborative process of developing the vision and a shared mission statement is critical to the long-term success of any school. The vision, however, must evolve out of the lives and philosophies of the educators involved, not just out of committee consensus. All decisions made about the school should be guided by a shared vision and the living, breathing mission statement derived from that vision.

The mission statement should take into account the district philosophy and goals as well as relevant state and federal guidelines. Data from national studies and local action research studies provide further information about promising practices. School leaders keep their fingers on the school's pulse and regularly ask for input into the vision and mission statement from students, parents, and community. The fundamental building block, however, must always be the very best knowledge we have about the human growth and development of youngsters ages 10 to 15.

When a shared vision and mission statement become operational, middle level educators pursue appropriate practices in developing a challenging academic program; they develop criteria to guide decisions and a process to make needed changes. Reviewing new ideas as they apply to this vision and its subsequent mission is a task that must be revisited regularly as circumstances change and new research and practices emerge.

An inviting, supportive, and safe environment

A successful school for young adolescents is an inviting, supportive, and safe place, a joyful community that promotes in-depth learning and enhances students' physical and emotional well-being. In a healthy school environment, human relationships are paramount.

Visitors see staff members who are cordial to each other, teachers and administrators who speak to students by name, and students who interact comfortably and respectfully with adults and each other. Statements of encouragement and positive feedback substantially outnumber disciplinary or correctional comments. Interactions among staff members and between students reflect democracy, fairness, and mutual respect. Teachers, staff, and students learn and put into practice the skills of direct feedback, mediation, healthy and appropriate confrontation, positive risk taking, and personal and collaborative goal setting. Students and adults have a shared language to discuss issues of diversity and equity. The essence of a happy, healthy school lies in the talk one hears.

Everyone in an inviting school works proactively to eliminate harassment, verbal abuse, bullying, and name-calling. Students and teachers understand that they are part of a community where differences are respected and celebrated. When this egalitarian concept becomes embedded in daily school life, less time is devoted to settling disputes and managing classroom discipline. In schools that promote a safe and supportive environment, students are encouraged to take intellectual risks, to be bold with their expectations, and to explore new challenges. Every student – no matter what creed, color, or uniqueness – serves as a genuine part of the community and contributes based on individual strengths.

The team is a home away from home, the place where students work and learn together with teachers and classmates with whom they identify.

The school ensures that every student has at least one adult advocate who knows that student well, and all students are comfortable talking to any staff member. Schools develop structures so that students will be known as individuals and feel cared for and valued. Teams comprised of two or more teachers with the students they teach in common are essential to the process of creating learning communities. The team is a home away from home, the place where students work and learn together with teachers and classmates with whom they identify.

The school buildings and campus make an immediately visible statement about caring. An attractive, inviting, and clean physical plant is an expression of a supportive and safe environment. Student work is prominently displayed, an indication that learning is a school priority. Like the young adolescents themselves, the climate of developmentally responsive middle level schools requires constant nurturing.

Middle level educators, students, and their families plan and implement effective transition procedures for incoming students. These activities ensure that students become successfully integrated into the middle level school and maintain their continuous academic and social progress. Transition activities for students moving to the next level must be planned collaboratively with high school educators who recognize, understand, and build on the strong preparation students have received.

High expectations for every member of the learning community

Educators in developmentally responsive middle level schools hold and act upon high expectations for themselves as well as their students. Likewise, students hold themselves and their teachers to equally high expectations. Such confidence promotes positive attitudes and behaviors and motivates students to tackle challenging learning activities. Teachers convey their high expectations by personal examples, gestures, casual remarks, and attitudes.

> Successful middle level schools are grounded in the understanding that young adolescents are capable of far more than adults often assume.

Successful middle level schools are grounded in the understanding that young adolescents are capable of far more than adults often assume. Educators recognize that students are curious and concerned about the world and their place in it, and they understand that students thrive when engaging in genuine activities that make a difference in their schools and communities. Young adolescents need adults who believe in them and provide appropriate challenges, opportunities, and support.

Achieving high academic performance for every student requires more than just raising standards or gaining an adequate score on a standardized test. It means empowering students to learn, to become intellectually engaged, and to behave as responsible citizens. It calls for them to develop initiative and responsibility so they can reach their potential. High expectations require adults to start where students are, understanding their individual needs, interests, and learning styles, then fashion a substantive curriculum and pace for learning to accomplish individual levels of understanding and development. In this way, educators translate expectations into standards that are concrete, clearly written with examples, congruent with a school's mission, and frequently revisited.

Adults and young people alike tend to live up to these expectations. Where teachers expect much of themselves, there is every likelihood they will not be disappointed when they expect much of young adolescents.

Students and teachers engaged in active learning

Successful middle schools are characterized by the active engagement of students and teachers. It could not be otherwise, for everything we know about the nature of young adolescents and the principles of learning makes it obvious that the most successful learning strategies are ones that involve each student personally. Developmentally responsive instructional practices place students at the center of the learning process. In such situations students are viewed as actors rather than audience.

The intellectual development that occurs between the years 10 to 15 permits students to become more active participants in the teaching-learning process. As they gradually develop the ability to hypothesize, to organize information into useful and meaningful constructs, and to grasp long-term cause and effect relationships, students are ready and able to play a major role in their own learning and education.

Although hands-on activities are universally advocated, developmentally responsive middle schools take that concept further with what might be termed "hands-joined" activities, ones teachers and students develop by working together. Such activities promote student ownership and lead to levels of understanding and motivation unlikely when students are simply completing teacher-made assignments.

When students routinely assume the role of teacher, and teachers demonstrate that they are still learners, the conditions of a genuine learning community are present. Teachers are active participants in learning activities rather than just being observers of students at work. Such collaboration leads to mastery of important concepts, demonstrates democratic processes, and fosters meaningful student-teacher relationships.

An adult advocate for every student

Academic success and personal growth increase markedly when young adolescents' affective needs are met. Therefore, all adults in developmentally responsive middle level schools are advocates, advisors, and mentors. The concept of advocacy is fundamental to the school's culture, embedded in its every aspect. Advocacy is not a singular event or a regularly scheduled time; it is an attitude of caring that translates into action when adults are responsive to the needs of each and every young adolescent in their charge.

> Young adolescents have many concerns about matters that lie outside the parameters of the academic curriculum, and they need opportunities to discuss these with one another and a trusted adult.

Each student must have one adult to support that student's academic and personal development. This adult is a model of good character who is knowledgeable about young adolescent development in general, who self-evidently enjoys working with young adolescents, and who comes to know students well as individuals. Advocates or advisors are not counselors, but they listen and guide youth through the ups and downs of school life. Young adolescents have many concerns about matters that lie outside the parameters of the academic curriculum, and they need opportunities to discuss these with one another and a trusted adult.

The advisor is the primary liaison between the school and family and often initiates contact with parents, providing pertinent information about the student's program and progress, as well as being ready to receive calls from any parent with a concern. Helping families stay engaged in their child's education is a critical task. Students seeking independence often prefer to keep home and school separate, but a high quality of three-way communication will ensure that students, their parents, and the advisor will be mutually supportive.

Advisors are in a position to recognize behavioral changes in students that should be brought to the attention of counselors, administrators, teachers, parents, and others who could provide appropriate support. Advisors and all staff members facilitate healthy and caring peer relationships by modeling the interpersonal relationships that define the school vision. Protecting young adolescents from bullying, for instance, begins when teachers in their classrooms as well as the total culture of the school promote compassion, understanding, and mutual respect.

To assist teachers in fulfilling the pastoral role, middle level schools use a variety of organizational arrangements such as advisory programs, extended homerooms, and team-based mentorships. These efforts augment but do not conflict with comprehensive, essential guidance and support services. The successful school demonstrates a continuity of caring and support that extends throughout a student's middle level experience.

School-initiated family and community partnerships

Schools do not presume to educate children alone. In today's society, genuine family and community involvement are fundamental components of successful schools for young adolescents. Too many parents mistakenly become less involved in middle school, believing that their children need less support at this level. Continuing parental involvement is as important as ever, so schools must take the initiative to develop needed home-school bonds. Frequently parents are uncertain about how they can be involved in this new and often larger school. They may also be unsure about the most appropriate way to deal with their rapidly changing and maturing child but are hesitant to seek assistance.

Research studies clearly link the involvement of both family and other adults in the community with higher levels of student achievement, improved student behavior, and greater overall support for schools. Successful middle level schools, therefore, promote family involvement by sponsoring parent education programs, creating and maintaining links between home and school, initiating volunteer programs, establishing coordinated home-school learning experiences, and developing activities that involve community businesses and various cultural and civic groups.

Principals and faculty members in these schools use a variety of ways to reach out to families in partnership including meeting in community centers or local housing projects, using language interpreters, or setting up a school "Family Learning Center" where parents can obtain information, have materials translated, or meet with school officials and other parents. The traditional practices of school newsletters, report cards, and parent-teacher conferences have been joined and enhanced by e-mail, Web sites, student-led conferences, and homework hotlines as valuable communication tools to inform and involve parents and community members.

Middle level schools also seek appropriate partnerships with businesses, social service agencies, and other organizations whose purposes are consistent with the school's mission. Students become involved in apprenticeships, shadow studies, service learning projects, and activities that use the community as a learning site. Community members and school partners can provide considerable assistance and expertise in the school's instructional program as well.

In any partnership or venture, all parties must benefit and share mutually understood roles and expectations. The school-family-community relationship is no different. Schools should expect families and community to take advantage of opportunities provided to support student learning. Further, families should spend time engaged in their children's learning, thus demonstrating belief in the importance of school success. When collaborating with families, educators must be sensitive to local and cultural considerations.

Successful schools for young adolescents provide

Curriculum that is relevant, challenging, integrative, and exploratory

Curriculum is the primary vehicle for achieving the goals and objectives of a school. As commonly conceived, curriculum refers to the content and skills taught. In developmentally responsive middle level schools, however, curriculum embraces every planned aspect of a school's educational program. It includes those specific classes designed to advance skills and knowledge as well as school-wide services and programs such as guidance, clubs and interest groups, music and drama productions, student government, sports, and service learning experiences.

An effective middle level curriculum is distinguished by learning activities that appeal to young adolescents and create opportunities to pose and answer questions that are important to them. The curriculum of a successful middle level school must be relevant, challenging, integrative, and exploratory, from both the student's as well as the teacher's perspective.

In exemplary middle level schools, curriculum is planned in units that last several weeks, using complex tasks and essential questions rather than day-to-day lessons. These units are often organized around a theme or integrated by a melding of the teacher goals and students' questions rather than through the separate subject format more appropriate for high schools.

The "hidden curriculum," what students learn indirectly from the people they come in contact with, the structures in which they work, and the issues that inevitably occur in a human enterprise, has a powerful influence on what students learn. In fact, this aspect of learning is sometimes so profound and long-lasting that it overrides more traditional learning. Lives are shaped less by direct instruction than by "wayside teaching," those small individual actions, probing questions, subtle reminders, earned commendations, and personalized challenges. Teachers in successful middle level schools skillfully interweave the planned curriculum with the unplanned, ensuring that interactions with students are positive, all students are valued, and all students are treated equitably.

> **The "hidden curriculum" has a powerful influence on what students learn.**

The age-old but recently reinforced task of covering prescribed content constitutes an ongoing challenge for middle level teachers and curriculum developers since they recognize that covering and learning are not synonymous. The task of designing developmentally appropriate educational experiences for young adolescents that takes into account state and federal standards is a challenge worthy of our best efforts.

Relevant

Curriculum is relevant when it allows students to pursue answers to questions they have about themselves, content, and the world. When teachers help them see the many connections that link various subjects, students recognize the holistic nature of all knowledge. Student-generated questions may lead to more demanding study, particularly when the prescribed curriculum is too often preoccupied with answers to questions young adolescents never ask. They need opportunities to study concepts and learn skills in areas that interest them as well as those determined by adults. Almost any aspect of a school's curriculum may be relevant to a young adolescent when developed with reference to students' questions, ideas, and concerns. The more engaged and self-directed the youngster, the wider becomes what is "relevant." Relevant curriculum involves students in activities that are rich in personal meaning. Making curriculum relevant, however, does not by any means indicate topics and material to be studied should be limited solely to students' preexisting interests. Relevant curriculum creates new interests, opening doors to new knowledge and opportunities for "stretching" students to new levels of learning.

Challenging

Challenging curriculum actively engages young adolescents, marshalling their sustained interests and efforts. It addresses substantive issues and skills, is geared to their levels of understanding, and increasingly enables them to assume control of their own learning. Learning tasks must be perceived as achievable, even if difficult.

Emphasizing important ideas and skills requires teachers to stretch themselves, moving well beyond merely "covering material." Using their good judgment in consultation with students, they select ideas for in-depth study from a vast range of information and materials that are genuinely important and worth knowing. For these issues to come alive, teachers must help students examine values, assumptions, basic principles, and alternative points of view, addressing *why* things happen as well as *how.* They must teach skills and concepts in context, with the focus on helping students become skilled writers, thinkers, and explorers, rather than merely copying or memorizing others' ideas.

Given the developmental diversity present in any middle level classroom, gearing curriculum to each student's level of understanding can be a daunting task. In addition to varied learning styles and different rates of development, young adolescents' cultural backgrounds and prior experiences must be taken into account. Efforts to eliminate tracking and to include those with special needs in regular classes increase student diversity further. Adapting curriculum so as to challenge and provide continuous progress for each and every student requires significant collaboration among all teachers, counselors, school social workers, parents, and students.

Both content and methods must be diversified and individualized. As a first step, teachers can offer choices among learning opportunities, providing challenges for all students to reach and grow, whatever their current abilities. Independent study, small group work, special interest experiences, and apprenticeships are other means of addressing individual needs.

Because of young adolescents' drive toward independence, they need a challenging curriculum that ultimately enables them to guide the course of their own education. Consonant with their varying capacities to handle responsibility, students must be nurtured in making choices and decisions about curricular goals, content, activities, and means of assessment. In addition, every middle level student should have opportunities to participate in team governance that fosters initiative, responsibility, and understanding of and appreciation for a democratic way of life.

Integrative

Curriculum is integrative when it helps students make sense of their lives and the world around them and when students learn how to make significant, meaningful decisions about their learning. Such curriculum is coherent, focusing on those ideas that cross arbitrary subject boundaries.

Middle level schools must provide experiences, courses, and units, directed either by individual teachers or by teams, that are specifically designed to be integrative; for that is how young adolescents learn best. Reading, writing, and other fundamental skills should be taught and practiced wherever they apply, rather than taught only in isolation as separate subjects. Moreover, all teachers should help students see how content and skills learned in school are applicable in their daily lives. Using journals, portfolios, conferences, and other strategies provide students opportunities to reflect on their experiences, an essential step toward recognizing their progress and accepting responsibility for their own learning. Reflection is a natural part of self-evaluation and ongoing learning.

Integrating all these dimensions is most effective when the curriculum is focused on issues significant to both students and adults. Since real life issues are by nature transdisciplinary, attention to them integrates the curriculum in natural ways. Intellectual, social, physical, communication, and technological skills are learned and applied in context. Critical thinking, decision making, and creativity are enhanced when students examine appropriate problems and take steps to help solve them. In such cases, they produce or construct knowledge rather than simply being consumers of information.

> Since real life issues are by nature transdisciplinary, attention to them integrates the curriculum in natural ways.

Exploratory

The middle school is the finding place. The entire curriculum at this level should be exploratory, for young adolescents, by nature, are adventuresome, curious explorers. Exploration, in fact, is the aspect of a successful middle school's curriculum that most directly and fully reflects the nature and needs of young adolescents. Although some experiences or courses may be labeled exploratory, it should not be assumed they are, therefore, non-academic. The reverse is also true; a solid academic, science for example, when properly taught, clearly is exploratory. Exploration is an attitude and approach, not a classification of content.

There is a particularly critical side to the exploratory responsibility of the middle level. In many respects, this level of school is a last chance. If youth pass through early adolescence without broad, exploratory experiences, their future lives may be needlessly restricted.

They deserve opportunities to ascertain their special interests and aptitudes, to engage in activities that will broaden their views of the world and of themselves. They need, for instance, the chance to be a member of a musical group, though never destined to become a professional musician, to have a part in a play, though never to become an actor, or to create visual images through drawing and painting, though never to become an artist.

Curriculum that is exploratory also has potential career value, leads to healthy recreational and leisure time pursuits, or is a precursor for significant community service. It enriches life and makes a major contribution to the development of well-rounded, more self-sufficient adults. Exploratory and enrichment experiences are fundamental components of a successful middle level school and deserve full attention.

Curriculum for the 21st Century

The middle level curriculum needed today must respond to more demands than ever, including newer state and federal standards. However, that does not mean the curriculum should be standardized or uninspired. Curriculum that meets the needs of young adolescents is based on criteria of high quality that provide direction for what young adolescents should know and be able to do and help them achieve the attitudes and behaviors needed for a full, productive, and satisfying life. Such a curriculum seeks to achieve objectives that go well beyond scores on standardized tests.

Developing curriculum is an important responsibility for educators who must cultivate the disposition and skills of scholarship and provide learning experiences that draw from and integrate the disciplines. The rapid expansion of knowledge constitutes the ongoing and difficult task of selecting content that is at the same time relevant, challenging, integrative, and exploratory. No other phase of designing a successful middle school is as important as creating developmentally responsive curriculum.

Multiple learning and teaching approaches that respond to their diversity

The distinctive developmental and learning characteristics of young adolescents provide the foundation for selecting learning and teaching strategies, just as they do for designing curriculum. Teaching approaches should enhance and accommodate the diverse skills, abilities, and prior knowledge of young adolescents, cultivate multiple intelligences, and draw upon students' individual learning styles. Students should acquire various ways of posing and answering questions and engage in learning situations wherein basic skills are mastered in functional contexts. When learning experiences capitalize on students' cultural, experiential, and personal backgrounds, new concepts are built on knowledge students already possess. Advancing every student's literacy and numeracy development is an ongoing, faculty-wide responsibility embedded in the curriculum.

Since young adolescents learn best through engagement and interaction, learning strategies involve students in dialogue with teachers and with one another. They participate in decisions about what to study and how best to study the topics selected. While some direct, teacher-centered instruction is in order, varied approaches are needed including experiments, demonstrations, surveys and opinion polls, simulations, inquiry-based and group projects, and independent study. Individual differences are accommodated through abundant opportunities for student choice within classes and co-curricular programs. Experiences are provided that appeal to students with special talents or interests – intellectual, athletic, or artistic.

Teachers of various specialties work together to design learning activities that will ensure appropriate challenges for all types of learners. Emphasis is on collaboration and cooperation. Varying forms of group work are used, depending on the purpose, with students at different times clustered at random by ability, by interest, or by other criteria, always with the goal of increasing student engagement and learning. School personnel work in partnership with the families of special needs students to determine the best educational program.

Instructional materials and resources are most worthwhile when they provide multiple viewpoints and encourage young adolescents to explore new ideas. The library-media specialist assists teachers and teams by providing supplementary print and non-print resources related to topics being investigated. The community is a major resource, serving both as a site for learning experiences that cannot be provided in a classroom and as a source of materials and guest experts for class activities.

> **Instructional materials and resources are most worthwhile when they provide multiple viewpoints and encourage young adolescents to explore new ideas.**

Technology should be used to advance learning and should be available to every student. It is not an end in itself but opens up new instructional and learning opportunities. Technology can develop higher-order thinking skills and provide the most current information from many sources, enabling teachers and students to interact with real world resources in unprecedented ways. Through professional development educators must become proficient in integrating technology into the curriculum. Properly used, technology also helps students develop personal responsibility and independence and prepares them for contemporary life. Finally, although already comfortable with technology, students need to investigate the many ramifications of what it means to live in a technological society and become informed and wise consumers of modern media.

Major learning activities or units should always culminate in some form of presentation in which students share with their parents and others what they have done and learned. Learning approaches that are developmentally responsive require students to set personal goals and consider their progress in achieving both the knowledge and behavioral goals consistent with applicable standards.

Assessment and evaluation programs that promote quality learning

Continuous, authentic, and appropriate assessment and evaluation measures provide evidence about every student's learning progress. Such information helps students, teachers, and family members select immediate learning goals and plan further education. Grades alone are inadequate expressions for assessing and reporting student progress on the many goals of middle level education. In fact, grades may actually work to inhibit many students' learning and development, forcing them to compete in an unequal race they know they cannot win.

Students should have opportunities to set personal goals, chart their individual growth, and reflect on their progress in achieving the knowledge, skill, and behavioral objectives of education. Means of assessing student progress should also serve a learning function, helping students to clarify their understandings as well as providing information on which to make a judgment.

Although the words are often used interchangeably, *assessment* and *evaluation* are distinctly different functions. Assessment is the process of estimating a student's progress toward an objective and using that information to help students continue their learning. Evaluation is the process of using data and standards to judge the quality of progress or level of achievement. Assessment and evaluation should include both the processes and the products of learning, taking into account student differences.

Teachers should specify the criteria for evaluation in advance in the form of a rubric that defines levels of quality. These rubrics should be designed with appropriate student involvement. Examples of quality work should be readily available. Young adolescents are capable of being active participants in both assessment and evaluation and judging their accomplishments.

In addition to the content knowledge and skills typically evaluated through paper and pencil tests, ways of assessing and evaluating students' growth must address the many other aspects of a student's development including critical thinking, independence, responsibility, and those other desired personal attributes and dispositions that have lifelong influence. This requires a variety of assessment strategies including journals, electronic portfolios, demonstrations, peer feedback, teacher-designed tests, and audio or video evidences of learning.

In developmentally responsive middle level schools, assessment and evaluation procedures also reflect the characteristics and uniqueness of young adolescents. Since early adolescence is a crucial period in building a clear self-concept and positive self-regard, assessment and evaluation should emphasize individual progress rather than comparison with other students and should not rely on extrinsic motivation. The goal is to help students discover and understand their strengths, weaknesses, interests, aptitudes, and personalities. Student self-assessment helps develop a fair and realistic self-concept. Young adolescents' concern with peer approval is another reason to emphasize individualized evaluation and minimize comparisons with others.

Educators should recognize students' efforts and support their developing work ethic, knowing that all students cannot reach a uniform standard at the same time. Emphasis should be on what the student has accomplished. Successful schools also help families see how a student's performance corresponds with national or state norms.

Young adolescents' desire for independence often leads to breakdowns in communication with adults in the family. However, when students, families, and the teaching team all have active roles in evaluating student progress, that gap is bridged. Student-led conferences are especially valuable in achieving the goals of an assessment and reporting program. Various kinds of written reports from both students and teachers, plus telephone and e-mail messages keep home and school working together. Web sites provide opportunities for parents, teachers, and students to connect electronically, promoting continuous communication between home and school.

Organizational structures that support meaningful relationships and learning

The ways schools organize teachers and schedule and group students have a significant impact on the learning environment. The interdisciplinary team of two to four teachers working with a common group of students is the signature component of high-performing schools, literally the heart of the school from which other desirable programs and experiences evolve. Although sometimes perceived primarily as an organizational arrangement, teaming must be much more. Teaming is the starting place for building a strong learning community with its sense of family, where students and teachers know one another well, feel safe and supported, and are encouraged to take intellectual risks.

> The interdisciplinary team is the signature component of high-performing schools, literally the heart of the school.

Research shows that effective teams lead to improved student achievement, increased parental contacts, an enhanced school climate, and positive student attitudes. Smaller teams of two or three teachers have proven to be especially effective in achieving these benefits. Furthermore, teaming has a positive impact on the professional lives of teachers, improving their sense of accomplishment. Whether organized formally as vertical teams or not, teachers of a particular subject have regular opportunities to meet together.

Daily or regular common planning time is essential so that teams can plan ways to integrate the curriculum, analyze test data, review student work, discuss current research, and reflect on the effectiveness of instructional approaches. Addressing the concerns of individual students and day-to-day management details are important topics on a team's agenda but should not consume the bulk of common planning time.

To achieve a desired sense of smallness, large schools may be subdivided into "houses" or "schools-within-a-school." Either option can replicate on a smaller scale the same mix of grade levels, ethnic groups, and socioeconomic status that makes up the school as a whole. Such arrangements foster the long-term student-teacher relationships known to have real value during these transition years, from both an educational and developmental standpoint. Keeping a small team of teachers and their students together for two or three years – a process often referred to as looping – and organizing a multiage team comprised of two or three grade levels have demonstrated their merit. These arrangements, which harken back to the one-room school, deserve serious consideration because of their value in promoting students' overall development and learning.

Daily or regular common planning time is essential so teams can plan ways to integrate the curriculum, analyze test data and student work, and discuss current research and instructional approaches.

A schedule that provides large blocks of class time permits teaching teams to conduct valuable learning experiences such as field trips, debates, mock trials, or science experiments that are not possible in the usual single period. In such a block schedule, a few students can be provided remedial support or others freed to do enrichment activities without interfering with the ongoing program. On occasion, two or three teams or an entire grade level can meet together during the block.

Recognizing the limiting and many negative effects of academic tracking, successful middle level schools use enrichment programs, cooperative learning groups, independent study, and other practices that respond to the variety of student competencies, interests, and abilities and meet the needs of advanced learners.

In exemplary middle level schools, teachers who work together on a team design and operate much of the program, collaborating across teaching specialties, sharing responsibility for literacy development, advocacy, and student life. They take advantage of opportunities to vary the use of time, space, staff, and grouping arrangements to achieve success for every student. Team leaders represent their teams on a school-wide leadership team where they work with administrators to set direction, provide feedback, and evaluate the school.

School-wide efforts and policies that foster health, wellness, and safety

Developmentally responsive middle level schools promote abundant opportunities for students to develop and maintain healthy minds and bodies and to understand their personal growth. An emphasis on health, wellness, and safety permeates the entire school, with faculty members sharing responsibility for maintaining a positive school environment. The risks associated with tobacco, alcohol, drugs, diets, and sexual activities are addressed in such a school.

A coordinated health program concentrates on those areas of students' personal lives that enhance or interfere with learning. These areas provide opportunities for developing and practicing healthful decision-making, coping, and refusal skills that are purposely reinforced throughout the curriculum. Written policies support and direct a school's efforts to address health and wellness within courses, the school culture, school and community collaborative projects, and parent partnerships. All adults are encouraged to model good health habits. Local health agencies cooperate with school and families in dealing with young adolescent health issues. Schools actively promote a safe and welcoming environment by developing school and community-wide initiatives that identify risks and promote protective conditions through a true home-school-community partnership.

> **The school emphasizes lifelong physical activities such as aerobics, dance, and leisure-time sports and fitness programs.**

A comprehensive health and wellness program includes student-focused, integrated experiences that are implemented throughout the curriculum, plus daily physical education activities that improve students' cardiovascular fitness, coordination, agility, and strength. The school emphasizes lifelong physical activities such as aerobics, dance, and leisure-time sports and fitness programs. Intramural and extra-curricular activities that require physical activity must be developmentally appropriate, be open to the entire student body, and comply with recognized national standards. Schools also recognize students for gains they make toward personal goals based on individual wellness profiles.

A school that fosters physical and psychological safety strives to build resiliency in young people by maintaining an environment in which peaceful and safe interactions are expected and supported by written policies, scheduled professional development, and student-focused activities. These policies are clearly communicated to students, teachers, and families. A strong sense of school community is developed by teaching students how to manage anger, resolve conflicts peacefully, and prevent hateful or violent behaviors.

Schools whose policies, professional development plans, and both formal and informal curricula consistently address the issues mentioned previously will also succeed in fostering health, wellness, and safety. In such schools students have an increased sense of well-being and a greater likelihood of succeeding academically.

Multifaceted guidance and support services

Young adolescents live in a world that presents them with many choices. Developmentally responsive middle level schools, therefore, provide both teachers and specialized professionals who are readily available to offer the assistance many students need in negotiating their lives both in and out of school. Counselors, special needs teachers, school psychologists, social workers, school nurses, and community liaisons assist young adolescents with learning difficulties, social adjustments, family issues, and health problems. They use their specific knowledge and skills to team with classroom teachers and administrators to promote student

> Developmentally responsive middle level schools provide the assistance many students need in negotiating their lives both in and out of school.

progress. Consistent communication and interaction among specialists and classroom teachers help to assure that student behaviors and
learning needs are accurately assessed and met. All faculty are aware
of appropriate referral services and procedures to follow when rec-
ommending students for specialized services.

Counselors, administrators, and teachers can
use student advocacy programs to provide ongoing
assistance to all students. These programs make it
possible for concerned adults to meet regularly with
students in small groups during the school day.
Small partner teams are especially effective in providing classroom-based guidance and support. Advocacy programs help students develop respect for
self and others. They foster compassion, a workable
set of values, and the skills of cooperation, decision making, and goal
setting. The advocacy program design is based on the specific culture
of the school and community and is developed to meet the needs of
those particular students. Advocates receive ongoing professional development to help fulfill this vital role.

> Advocacy programs help students develop respect for self and others. They foster compassion, a workable set of values, and the skills of cooperation, decision making, and goal setting.

School counselors support teachers in advisory programs, demonstrate and conduct classroom group activities, and offer both one-
on-one and small group guidance sessions for students as needed.
They sponsor peer mediation and peer tutoring programs and share
their expertise with teams and individual teachers, often serving as
resource persons in classroom activities. They also meet with parents,
usually in conjunction with teams or individual teachers.

Parents need help in understanding the relationship between
various middle school course options and the high school's programs.
School counselors facilitate transition programs for students entering
and exiting the middle level school. An essential part of that transition
is identifying special needs students and communicating their assistance plans to those responsible for them.

School counselors coordinate the support services provided by the school system, ensuring the most effective use of specialists such as school psychologists, social workers, and speech therapists. They see that guidance services are articulated with those of the district's elementary and high schools and access and coordinate community-based services for the well-being of their students. Counselors are important specialists with people-oriented skills and should not be burdened with administrative or report-related responsibilities.

In Retrospect

The importance of middle level education can never be over-estimated. Lives are at stake. Creating schools able to adequately fulfill the broad responsibilities that the middle level inevitably carries requires expansive support. Such support from the profession as well as the general population must evolve from a full understanding of young adolescents and an appreciation of the importance of the educational experiences they undergo. Yet the public and many educators have a very limited understanding of the nature and needs of young adolescents and the types of educational programs that are best suited for them during the stage of life between the ages of 10 and 15.

Therefore, National Middle School Association has set forth its vision in this document. This position paper embodies the educational ideals that comprise the middle school concept. The nature of the conditions that should prevail in a middle school in order for it to be successful are presented. The practices advocated rest on and are derived from a foundation comprised of what is known about young adolescents and the accepted principles of learning. While grade configurations may vary, the nature of the program provided youth is the crucial factor.

Because a full understanding of the developmental characteristics of young adolescents is so important, information about the age group has been included in an introductory section and in many references throughout. In addition, a major research-supported and thorough treatment of the characteristics of these distinctive young people has been presented in a concluding section. These important materials should be referenced regularly by parents as well as educators. Decisions about programs and strategies should always be measured against the yardstick of this understanding.

As one pauses to contemplate the message of this important document, the need for various stakeholders to take positive, proactive steps becomes paramount. The Call to Action that follows provides specific charges to various constituencies, all of whom have roles to play in improving the education of young adolescents. Middle level schools are in a particularly critical position because of the opportunity they have to influence, for better or worse, not only the students themselves but society at large. The future for our society hangs in the balance.

Call to Action

*T*his We Believe: Successful Schools for Young Adolescents is a strong statement about the nature of exemplary middle level schools. It should be circulated widely as should the companion volume *Research and Resources in Support of This We Believe.* To ensure the implementation of the position paper's advocacies, however, requires action on the part of many individuals, groups, and agencies. Use these major documents to revitalize efforts to improve middle schools in ways known to be compatible with human growth and development and accepted principles of learning. No matter what your role, there are steps that any individual with a stake in middle level education can take. You can readily find a category, often more than one, to match your status and identify specific actions that you can and should take.

Teachers:

- Become personally familiar with the contents of this position paper, studying it sufficiently so that its positions are understood and you can converse with others about the document.

- Familiarize yourself with the organization and content of the companion volume, *Research and Resources.*

- Review your teaching style and methods, noting where your practices do not seem to match the paper's advocacies. Review the research reported that deals with areas where changes in your methods should be considered.

- With your team discuss the various suggestions about teaming to determine which of your practices match or deviate from what is envisioned.

- Designate two team meetings a month to discuss the implications of the sections on curriculum and multiple learning and teaching approaches. Follow those meetings with discussions focused on assessment and organizational structures.

- Enlist a colleague to make targeted classroom observations of your teaching.

- Consider ways you could be a better advocate for students, and also consider how the advisory program could be strengthened. Reflect anew on your importance as a model and example for the young adolescents you teach. Determine what changes your team can make to fulfill its advocacy role.

Principals:

- Become personally familiar with the contents of this paper, studying it sufficiently so that its positions are understood and you can converse with others about the document.

- Familiarize yourself with the organization and content of the companion volume, *Research and Resources.*

- Make an initial assessment of how your school rates on each of the 14 characteristics.

- Plan with the school's leadership team ways to use the two documents in upcoming professional development programs.

- Secure copies of both documents to place in the hands of each member of the board of education, the superintendent, and other appropriate central office personnel.

- Request an opportunity to meet with the superintendent to review the documents and discuss implications for your system.

- Schedule an appearance at a board of education meeting to highlight the document and its implications for your system. Prepare written materials to leave with members.

- Secure copies of the position paper to place in the hands of appropriate parent leaders.

- Consider organizing a cluster of principals in your area to discuss these documents and exchange ideas.

Parents:

- Read the position paper carefully in order to form an opinion about its guidelines and determine how the middle school's current program seems to match what the position paper advocates.

- Volunteer to participate on any committee or in any group that is or will be reviewing the middle school program. Accept all invitations offered by the school to attend meetings or school programs.

- Read some resources that seek to explain the age of early adolescence. If your middle school does not now have a collection of resources for parents, take the lead in establishing one.

- Organize and conduct one or more parent study groups to discuss the position paper.

- Ask to do a shadow study in the school to develop an understanding of the school day from a student's perspective.

- Work with other parent leaders to schedule an upcoming meeting for the parent-teacher-student organization to deal specifically with the position paper.

Superintendents:

- Read carefully and thoughtfully the entire position paper, considering the major recommendations that seem to conflict with the current program.

- Study the companion volume, *Research and Resources,* becoming sufficiently familiar with its contents and organization so you can reference it when needed.

- Share with your board of education copies of both documents and your belief in their importance as guidelines for establishing board policies relating to the middle level.

- Confer with the middle school principal(s) to determine how these documents can best be used in improving our middle school program.

- Contact the executive director of the state superintendents' group and plan ways for these documents to be publicized and shared in appropriate state newsletters and conferences.

- Contact the state superintendent of schools and/or the state department official charged with responsibility for middle level education to make sure that this person has copies of these documents and that copies will be made available to members of the state board of education and to key legislators.

Local and state boards of education, departments of education:
- Read the position paper carefully and discuss its implications for your school or state.

- Discuss your reactions with appropriate professional personnel.

- Set in motion a review of existing board policies that relate to the middle school as a first step in developing policies that are consistent with the advocacies of the position paper.

- Plan for a study of this document at a board of education retreat or special work session.

Teacher educators:
- Order several copies of both documents for the institution's library or curriculum center.

- Determine the best place in the undergraduate sequence to use one or both of these documents as supplementary texts.

- Identify the best places in the various graduate programs to use both documents as supplementary texts or required readings.

- Secure copies of both documents for the dean of education and other appropriate university officials. Send with a cover letter and follow up with a visit.

- Make sure the person designated for middle level education at the state department of education has copies of both documents.

- Plan with colleagues how the position paper can best be shared with the middle school teachers and administrators who cooperate with your teacher education program.

- Write a review or article about the position paper to submit to your state affiliate newsletter or journal.

- If your state does not now have distinctive middle level licensure, use this position paper as a way to initiate action with the state board and department of education.

- Regardless of state licensure, make sure your institution develops appropriate middle level courses and programs at both graduate and undergraduate levels.

- Contact the president or executive director of your state's association of teacher educators to plan for ways these documents can be brought to the attention of members.

- Develop a formal statement, in collaboration with the dean, expressing concern over the use of a single test as a determinant of a young adolescent's future. Submit such a statement to appropriate state level policymakers.

Characteristics of Young Adolescents

Youth between the ages of 10 to 15 are characterized by their diversity as they move through the pubertal growth cycle at varying times and rates. Yet as a group they reflect important developmental characteristics that have major implications for parents, educators, and others who care for them and seek to promote their healthy growth and positive development.

Following are what research suggests are notable characteristics of young adolescents in the physical, cognitive, moral, psychological, and social-emotional dimensions of development. Although most young adolescents in the United States will exhibit these characteristics to some degree, the relative importance of each characteristic can vary widely depending on the young adolescent. Gender, race, ethnicity and other cultural influences, family and economic situations, learning and physical disabilities, a young adolescent's temperament, and qualities of his or her community or neighborhood are just some of the factors that, working together, give these developmental dimensions and characteristics their personal and social meaning.

These characteristics also are presented in sequential fashion, but of course, they are not experienced in that way. Rather, all the dimensions are intertwined, each affecting and being affected by the others. For example, how young adolescents develop physically has ramifications for how they think of themselves psychologically and for how they interact socially with others. Because of many interconnections, the categories to which these developmental characteristics are assigned – psychological development rather than social-emotional, or cognitive rather than moral – are sometimes relatively arbitrary.

Young adolescents have a greater influence on their own developmental paths than they did in middle childhood. Most if not all of the characteristics highlighted here are the result of a give and take between the young adolescent and his or her ecology. These recurring interactions produce an infinite variety of developmental nuances that combine to reflect each young adolescent's unique personhood. So each of the characteristics listed here should be understood as a reasonable generalization for most young adolescents, but one that is more or less valid for particular young adolescents in particular situations.

In the area of *physical development,* young adolescents
- Experience rapid, irregular physical growth.

- Undergo bodily changes that may cause awkward, uncoordinated movements.

- Have varying maturity rates, with girls tending to begin puberty one and one-half to two years earlier than boys, and young adolescents in some cultural groups, such as African Americans, tending to begin puberty earlier than those in other groups.

- Experience restlessness and fatigue due to hormonal changes.

- Need daily physical activity because of increased energy, and if not actively engaged in regular physical activity, often lack fitness, with poor levels of endurance, strength, and flexibility.

- Need to release energy, often resulting in sudden, apparently meaningless outbursts of activity.

- Have preference for junk food but need good nutrition.

- May be prone to risky dieting practices, especially among European-American youth, in order to lose or gain weight.

- Continue to develop sexual awareness that increases with the onset of menstruation, the growth spurt, and the appearance of secondary sex characteristics.

- Are concerned with bodily changes that accompany sexual maturation and changes resulting in an increase in nose size, protruding ears, long arms, and awkward posture, concerns magnified because of comparison with peers.

- Have an increased need for comprehensive, medically accurate education about sexuality and health issues that responds to these increased concerns.

- Are physically vulnerable because they may adopt poor health habits or engage in experimentation with alcohol and other drugs and high-risk sexual behaviors.

In the area of ***cognitive-intellectual development,*** young adolescents
- Display a wide range of individual intellectual development.

- Increasingly are able to think abstractly, not only concretely; both concrete and abstract thinking styles may be in evidence in the same young adolescent, depending on the issue or situation.

- Commonly face decisions that require more sophisticated cognitive and social-emotional skills.

- Are intensely curious and have a wide range of intellectual pursuits, although few are – or need to be – sustained.

- Prefer active over passive learning experiences; depending on their cultural backgrounds; some young adolescents, such as Native American youth, may be quite engaged in learning through observation but not show this engagement through active participation.

- Prefer interaction with peers during learning activities.

- May show disinterest in conventional academic subjects but are intellectually curious about the world and themselves.

- Respond positively to opportunities to connect what they are learning to participation in real life situations, such as community service projects.

- Develop an increasingly more accurate understanding of their current personal abilities, but may prematurely close doors to future exploration in particular interest areas due to feeling inadequate in comparison to peers.

- Are developing a capacity to understand higher levels of humor, some of which may be misunderstood by adults to be overly sarcastic or even aggressive.

- Are inquisitive about adults and are keen observers of them; depending on their cultural upbringing, some young adolescents also may often challenge adults' authority.

In the area of *moral development,* young adolescents
- Are in transition from moral reasoning that focuses on "what's in it for me" to that which considers the feelings and rights of others; self-centered moral reasoning may be in evidence at the same time as other-or-principle-oriented reasoning, depending on the situation the young adolescent is in; in addition, cultural differences in the socialization of moral development, especially among young adolescents whose families are recent immigrants, may contribute to special moral conflicts or dilemmas for those young people attempting to navigate multiple cultures.

- Increasingly are capable of assessing moral matters in shades of grey as opposed to viewing them in black and white terms more characteristic of younger children; however, this increased potential for more complex moral reasoning may often not be evident in practice.

- Are generally idealistic, desiring to make the world a better place and to make a meaningful contribution to a cause or issue larger than themselves.

- Often show compassion for those who are downtrodden or suffering and have special concern for animals and the environmental problems that our world faces.

- Are capable of and value direct experience in participatory democracy.

- Owing to their lack of experience are often impatient with the pace of change, underestimating the difficulties in making desired social changes.

- Are likely to believe in and espouse values such as honesty, responsibility, and cultural acceptance, while at the same time learning that they and the people they admire also can be morally inconsistent, and can lie or cheat, avoid responsibility, and be intolerant.

- At times are quick to see flaws in others but slow to acknowledge their own faults.

- Are often interested in exploring spiritual matters, even as they may become distant from formal religious organizations; for many youth, however, especially African Americans, connection to religious organizations may continue to be a vital part of early adolescence.

- Are moving from acceptance of adult moral judgments to developing their own personal values; nevertheless, they tend to embrace major values consonant with those of their parents and other valued adults.

- Rely on parents and significant adults for advice, especially when facing major decisions.

- Greatly need and are influenced by trustworthy adult role models who will listen to them and affirm their moral consciousness and actions.

- Are increasingly aware of, concerned, and vocal about inconsistencies between values exhibited by adults and the conditions they see in society.

In the area of *psychological development,* young adolescents

- Are often preoccupied with self.

- Who have been socialized in European-American culture seek to become increasingly independent, searching for adult identity and acceptance, but they continue to need support and boundary-setting from adults; young adolescents from other cultural backgrounds, such as Hispanic or Asian American youth, may be as or more focused on their social obligations and roles in the family and other groups than they are on independence.

- May experience a significant increase in their awareness of, and the importance they give to, their ethnic identity.

- Experience levels of self-esteem that may fluctuate up and down, but in general are adequate and increase over time; in contrast, levels of belief in self-competence in academic subjects, sports, and creative activities often decline significantly from the levels of middle childhood.

- Believe that personal problems, feelings, and experiences are unique to themselves.

- Tend to be self-conscious and highly sensitive to personal criticism.

- Desire recognition for their positive efforts and achievements. Exhibit intense concern about physical growth and maturity as profound physical changes occur.

- Increasingly behave in ways associated with their sex as traditional sex role identification strengthens for most young adolescents; some young adolescents may question their sexual identities.

- Are curious about sex, and have sexual feelings; they need to know that these are normal.

- Are psychologically vulnerable, because at no other stage in development are they more likely to encounter and be aware of so many differences between themselves and others.

- Are also psychologically resilient; across diversities in race/ethnicity, residence, or socioeconomic status, young adolescents tend to be optimistic and have a generally positive view of their personal future.

In the area of *social-emotional development,* young adolescents

- Have a strong need for approval and may be easily discouraged.

- Are increasingly concerned about peer acceptance.

- Often overreact to ridicule, embarrassment, and rejection.

- Are dependent on the beliefs and values of parents and other valued adults, but seek to make more of their own decisions.

- Like fads, especially those shunned by adults.

- Have a strong need to belong to a group, with approval of peers becoming as important as adult approval, and on some matters even more important.

- Also need moderate amounts of time alone, in order to regroup and reflect on daily experiences.

- In their search for group membership, may experience significant embarrassment, ridicule, or rejection from those in other cliques from which they are excluded.

- Can gravitate toward affiliation with disruptive peers or membership in gangs in order to feel part of a group and to protect their physical safety.

- Experiment with new slang and behaviors as they search for a social position within their group, often discarding these "new identities" at a later date.

- Experience mood swings often with peaks of intensity and unpredictability.

- May exhibit immature behavior because their social skills and ability to regulate emotions frequently lag behind their cognitive and physical maturity; among some young adolescents, however, particularly those whose cultural backgrounds value such capacities, their social and emotional skills may be more advanced than their cognitive and physical maturity suggest.

- Must adjust to the social acceptance of early maturing girls and boys, especially if they themselves are maturing at a slower rate.

- If physically maturing earlier than peers, must deal with increased pressure around others' expectations of them, especially about engaging in high-risk behaviors.

- Often begin to experience feelings of sexual/romantic attraction to others, with some having significant sexual/romantic relationships, and a sizeable minority experiencing sexual behaviors.

- Often experience sexual harassment, bullying, and physical confrontations more than they did in elementary school or will in high school.

- Are often intimidated and frightened by their first middle level school experience because of the large numbers of students and teachers, the size of the building, and what may be for

many their first day-to-day experiences with significant pro-
portions of students who are culturally different from them.

- Are socially vulnerable, because, as they develop their beliefs, attitudes, and values, the emphasis media place on such
things as money, fame, power, and beauty (and the majority
culture perspectives which most often define those issues)
may negatively influence their ideals and values, or encourage them to compromise their beliefs.

This special section on the characteristics of young adolescents was
prepared by Dr. Peter C. Scales, Senior Fellow, Office of the President, Search Institute. Dr. Scales' recent research has focused on
identifying and promoting "developmental assets," those conditions
that are linked to young people's success in school and in life. Un-
fortunately, young people say they experience fewer of these assets
as they get older. Middle level educators are in a unique position to
help build many developmental assets such as feeling empowered and
playing useful roles, building social competence, and developing a
commitment to learning.

National Middle School Association

National Middle School Association, established in 1973, is the voice for professionals and others interested in the education and well-being of young adolescents. The association has grown rapidly and enrolls members in all 50 states, the Canadian provinces, and 42 other nations. In addition, 58 state, regional, and provincial middle school associations are official affiliates of NMSA.

NMSA is the only national association dedicated exclusively to the education, development, and growth of young adolescents. Membership is open to all. While middle level teachers and administrators make up the bulk of the membership, central office personnel, college and university faculty, state department officials, other professionals, parents, and lay citizens are members and active in supporting our single mission – improving the educational experiences of 10- to 15-year-olds. This open and diverse membership is a particular strength of NMSA's.

The association publishes *Middle School Journal,* the movement's premier professional journal; *Research in Middle Level Education Online; Middle Ground, the Magazine of Middle Level Education; Family Connection,* an online newsletter for families; *Classroom Connections,* a practical quarterly resource; and a series of research summaries.

A leading publisher of professional books and monographs in the field of middle level education, NMSA provides resources both for understanding and advancing various aspects of the middle school concept and for assisting classroom teachers in planning for instruction. More than 70 NMSA publications as well as selected titles published by other organizations are available through the resource catalog .

The association's highly acclaimed annual conference has drawn many thousands of registrants every fall. NMSA also sponsors many other professional development opportunities.

For information about NMSA and its many services, contact the association's headquarters office at 4151 Executive Parkway, Suite 300, Westerville, Ohio, 43081. TELEPHONE: 800-528-NMSA; FAX: 614-895-4750; INTERNET: www. nmsa.org.